The Wardrobe

Moya Pacey

The Wardrobe

Acknowledgements

'The Wardrobe' was shortlisted for the ACT David Campbell Prize 2008

'Insubordination' was Joint Winner of the
ACT Writers Centre Poetry Prize 2007

'Food of Love' was Winner of the
FAW Mornington Peninsula Poetry Prize 2008

'Wintergrief' was Commended in the Shoalhaven Poetry Awards 2006

Poems in this collection have appeared in *Poetrix*, *Island*,
The Canberra Times, *capital letters* and *Studio*

Thanks to Peter Bishop, Creative Director of Varuna,
for his trust in and encouragement of my poetry

For my family

The Wardrobe
ISBN 978 1 74027 580 4
Copyright © text Moya Pacey 2009
Cover photo used by permission of Memphis Vintage

First published 2009
Reprinted 2016

Ginninderra Press
PO Box 3461 Port Adelaide 5015
www.ginninderrapress.com.au

'Our passions do not live apart in locked chambers but dress in their small wardrobe of notions.'

George Eliot

Contents

On silent hold   9
- The Wardrobe   11
- Stealing Beauty   12
- Once upon a time   13
- Belfast Poem   14
- Cocktail cabinet   15
- The great loneliness   17
- In this place   18
- A yellow-eyed dog of a year   19
- Blood Ties   21
- Cornerstone   22
- Kitchen Ghosts   23
- Recipe for an apple cake   24

Disturbances   25
- This house is not quiet   27
- Green War   28
- It's too warm now for the bears to sleep   30
- Insubordination   31
- Cyberspeak   33
- White Dreams   34
- Dali Suite   35
- Take off your jacket   37
- Disapproval   38
- Whistling Shrimps   39
- Destruction of the Species   40
- At Darfur   41
- At the Liberty Hotel   42
- Food of Love   45
- On Figs   46

Poussins	48
Cordon Bleu	49
Of course it was over	50

Voyages   51

En route to Alaska	53
Riding the cable car	54
Tug of War Waikiki	55
Victoria Falls	56
Anzac Day at Moruya	57
Goosegreen	58
In the High Country	59
Detainees	60
Kaka	62
Kea	63
The Weight of Trees	64
A Tolstoy Reader in Melbourne	66
Trespassers	68
Evening Boat Ride on the Moruya River	70

Mysteries   71

A History of Birds	73
trust	74
Mothers Day	77
Singing Girl	78
76 Birkhall Road	79
Our Family Tree	81
Wintergrief	82
It seems he was loved until that moment	83
Soft Day	84
Prayer Bird	85

On silent hold

'and a wardrobe; … it did have its mysteries – …
everything always on silent hold.'
   from *Stepping Stones: Interviews with Seamus Heaney*
         by Dennis O'Driscoll, Faber & Faber 2008

The Wardrobe

A dress of turquoise like the sea
with silver threads and a skirt heavy

with the weight of silk.
High-heeled strappy shoes

for her dancing feet. A coat of
astrakhan impregnated with face powder

and Soir de Paris perfume.
In the pocket, a lipsticked handkerchief

lace-edged with a violet embroidered in one corner
and the letter 'P'; some copper coins

to spend a penny at the Astoria Dance Hall,
and a letter from a man whose name I do not remember.

Stealing Beauty

(for Catherine and MM)

You come home from Japan, bringing beauty;
I am sorry to rob you of it.
I tell you she is missing; gone for a whole night

and all of this morning, on her own hunt for beauty,
over the edge of the garden into the wild below.
We search and call; even the small children
next door look for her; ask where she is
I cannot tell.

I sit beneath your pohutukawa tree listening
for her bell; hearing only the tuis' frantic cries.
You say: it is not my fault that I have lost your cat.
'I know what she is like,' but I know this:

when she comes back that evening like a soft intruder
stealing in to surprise

                              she returns your beauty to you.

Once upon a time

You were five, wise, full of art and sing song
that summer lying in a string hammock
on the green wooden deck of the holiday house,
wearing orange goggles, your world squashed

luminous until the sun set the spotted
gums alight then drowned itself in the mangroves.
You slept; I crept to the ocean:
took soundings, noted rips, monitored sneaky

undertows, measured fast running currents,
dips, shifts, recorded all the fallings-off
flagged the shelves where dory shoals
slumbered unencumbered,

charted flights of silver gulls, observed
a lonely surfer leave the pewter sand
paddle far out back. Unwearied.
Home again, I whispered my map to you,

Stay safe my daring girl.
You woke then, and left in a blue car with fins.
Your hands were empty.
Your mouth was open in an 'O'.

Belfast Poem

(For Peggy)

In Belfast
you rolled away from me
so far
I was afraid you would fall
from that big soft bed.
Your breathing
scratchy, laboured.
Street noises at the window,
kids at play
like the summers of my childhood:
concrete street, running games;
Dad clipping his privet
hedging in my childhood.

Cocktail cabinet

I love to open it up;
pull down its heavy-hinged door
marvel at its interior brightly lit,
empty of cocktails.

It belongs in a smarter house
at the other end of town
where people have: drive ways,
garages, gardens with fountains;
and monkey puzzle trees.

At Christmas, my mother invites
the neighbours, opens it up;
reaches inside, pulls out a tumbler;
fills it to the brim –whiskey for Fred,
cream sherry for Vera.

She pours one for herself
in a mismatched glass. The one
with a flightless bird etched upon
its surface. As she sits, slowly
sipping, she transforms
becomes a screen siren – her favourite,
Rita Hayworth.

Instead of her jumper and skirt,
my mother is coiffured, jewelled;
softly perfumed, wearing a creation
designed by Dior, soft and silky
blackness, completely backless.

Haltered at the neck. A man's
manicured finger rests,
between her naked shoulder blades.
Clark Gable hands her a vodka cocktail.

The great loneliness

She's grown too old to sit at the table
tired of the paraphernalia of dining:
napkin rings, shining cutlery;
cruet sets. At breakfast, she balls her bread roll
into pellets, feeds them to sparrows
or the infestation of starlings
who come, just as daffodils have pushed
through after winter's gone.
Her daughter planted buckets of them
and a golden rose. She can't remember its name.
But it shows again and again.
Blooms all this last summer.

The man on the radio asks her to call him
with a story, or request a song;
she picks up the phone
worn to the colour of old bone,
presses it to her ear; stares,
catches the sun's last long rays.

These days she writes with a shaky finger
in the dust and grime on shelves.
'The world breaks and mends us.'

When the summer dark drifts down.
she sits in her red wing chair.
There's only a single light bulb
it's hard to see.
Outside, a sunflower in a terracotta pot surges.

In this place

In this place
bordered by the stark
edge of grief
air bites.

Earth has softened
and sticks to my boots.
Your grandson tidies
your grave
with tools from home.

Afterwards, he wipes them;
seals them in their plastic bag.
We leave a plant;
a special card.
Time muddies the message;
the plant freezes to death.

A yellow-eyed dog of a year

At the sharp, black rocks,
the man in the leather hat,
mirror glasses and a chin-strip beard
argues with his wife about the yellow-eyed dog.
'It's vicious,' she snarls.
'No way,' he barks. 'Timid more like.'
She ties it with a short lead.
It watches steady-eyed as the man
grim faced, baits his hooks ready
for rock fishing. The woman
takes their children and Needle,
a black, woolly-haired poodle, into the sea.
The yellow-eyed dog looks on;
pulls at its lead. Whimpers.

The man in the leather hat and the beard
looks over. I see me in his mirrors
my floppy pink hat
my green writing pad.
I know he wants me to leave.
I feel his ire from where I sit
sketching and scribbling.
So much so I have to stop.
Where did they come from
these spoilers?

Now, the yellow-eyed dog cries.
His family has moved away.
He tries to jump on the sand bank behind him.
He thinks he may be able to see them from there.
His paws cannot hold.
He cries louder.
Yelps.

I should untie him
take him to them.
Tell the bully with the mirror glasses,
Tie your dog where he can see you.

I wanted faraway peace
this last afternoon of the year;
I walked Shark Bay to get here.
The yellow-eyed dog and the spoilers
are at the blade end of the year's long argument.
I am tired of it.
In hours it will be history
the truce of a new year in its place.

When I risk a look behind, I see Needle,
the woolly black poodle has emerged from the sea.
He and the yellow-eyed dog are lying side by side;
I am going the wrong way.

Blood Ties

We stop by the coastal track.
A family swaddled by blood ties.
Behind us there's desert;
beside us there's water:
an ocean of it.

Keeping safe our secrets.
Keeping safe for our sakes.
Keepsakes.

Below us a brood of children
darts and scrambles
over the black rocks.
They are too far out;
their life lines snagged.
'Who will reel them in to safety?'
We can't.
Our lines are stretched too taut already.

Keeping safe our secrets.
Keeping safe for our sakes.
Keepsakes.

Cornerstone

By the lychgate, near a cypress hedge
where the scrunch of gravel
peters out, and pine needles drop
the sense of summer,
anchored beneath a wedge of shining stone,
there lies her husband.

She commissioned a master mason
to hew and heft a mausoleum
he finished with his chiselled
mark upon the lynchpin.

Inside the cathedral, a rose
window kaleidoscopes light.
Her wedding ring's stuck on a knuckled finger.
Her knees are flattened by the hassock of grief.

Kitchen Ghosts

Rene's at my side checking the jelly whip
A little more cream. Easy does it.
Just a drop.
Don't gild the lily.
Whip, whip, whip.

Whenever I boil a potato,
Charlie comes home wearing
that grey pullover with the beginnings
of a hole in the elbow, and no tie.
Irish eyes smiling – he steals
my heart away.
Give it back!

Panakalty calls Peggy,
'Corned beef stew sticks to your ribs.
Have you made plenty of gravy?'
Her sisters boil a pan full of green
cabbage with a ham bone in it.

Dympna buttons her coat; runs down
Agincourt Avenue to Sweeney's the bakers,
We'd rather miss daily mass than run out of soda bread.
Spread with butter from New Zealand
thick and for afters, tinned mandarin oranges

swimming like goldfish in a green glass bowl.
Sunday evening. Soft.
The wireless tuned in to *Sing Something Simple*.
'Turn it up,' Dad shouts,
'I can't hear a thing.

All this racket.
All I want is a quiet life.'

Recipe for an apple cake

Apples as green as hope fall at my feet
Windfalls begging for a little culinary magic.
Flour like hunger. Pure.
One egg from Bethany's hens laid this day
brown like wholemeal toast. I test its weight
crack open a miracle,
squawk of yellow white slides in
not wanting to be separated.
Like a favourite alliteration, butter rolls off my tongue.
Sugar like a memoir. *Those caramels of my childhood*
welded my milk teeth together.
Jug veined with age blue rimmed. Milk
brimmed. Lace doily weighed down with green glass beads
like courage. Keeps away summer flies. Buzz, buzz.
Pour the mixture into my grandmother's cake tin.
She left dents and a lifetime of filling bellies and social spaces.
Let it bake. Bring to the table
A poem you can eat.

Disturbances

'Humankind cannot bear very much reality'
 T.S. Eliot, 'Burnt Norton', from *Four Quartets*

This house is not quiet

(for Wallace Stevens)

This house is not quiet and the world is not calm.
This autumn night small animals are being harmed

by bigger ones in the violence of outside.
I am far away from quietude. My mind

is full of imperfections. I would rather live
through my body than through my mind.

Never read another word. My actions will be small.
I will do no harm; behave in a responsible way.

My gentle footprint, I'll leave on a beach to be washed
clean by a full-moon tide. When I swim, the ocean

will swim with me – there will be no resistance.
I want my house quiet and my world calm.

Green War

Citizens of the world, we are at war
Be on your guard
Wherever there is a vacant piece of land
Neglected
Forgotten
Our numbers will strike
Under cover of night.
Green fingered terrorists
Home grown
Armed with seed bombs
Pitchforks and manure,
We defy darkness:
Risk arrest
Scatter
French lavender
Paris Daisies
Welsh poppies
On your highway embankments.

Kamiyacho, Tokyo
Guerilla Gardeners numbers 1168 and 1169
grow their own sushi on waste ground:
pumpkins, radishes and broccoli;
wrap them in seaweed,
spot with pink ginger;
dabble wasabi.

Dublin, Ireland
Guerilla Gardener 2236
bombs the Luas Red Line
With nigella and hollyhock.
Shock and awe!

*Number 717 armed with an ice-cream scoop and fifty
crocus bulbs brings spring to South London.
Guerillas in Milan lob flower power bombs,
hurl earth and compost from cars and trains,
send green clematis climbing up telephone wires.
Belgium has gone green, issued
A Manifesto for the Sunflower,
and a Seed Grenade Instruction Manual.*

We are a secret world of green revolutionaries.
We will never surrender;
We will fight in our gardens
Defy the authorities
Declare death to the municipal
Uniformity of pansies and marigolds.
Our victory will be fragrant and nutritious.

It's too warm now for the bears to sleep

Weather always knows what it's about.
Snow has been falling in places where
it has never fallen before.
Seasons are dissolving
Sprinsumwintum.
It's already begun
golf balls
F a l l i   n g from the sky
Down they come
        o
        w
        n
scoring   a birdie.
There are no rules:
Ordinances,
Axioms,
Sutras
or Canons.
The bears have torn them up.

Insubordination

Father starts his campaign
razing the flower bed,
tossing last year's Summer Show
on the compost heap,
a yellowed dryness just
visible from the kitchen window.

Kitted out in his knife-edged gabardine,
raked and trowelled,
he orders me to prepare for
Next Season.
Earthworms are the first casualties,
wriggling a protest at their eviction.
A blackbird soon snaps them up.

I pour my winter sweat into the earth.
My father struts. 'Call that level?
Put some back bone into it, lad.'
Elbows me out of his way;
steps in to rig up his lines.

White string held taut. Whittled wash pegs
mark out His Territory.
He cuts open the seed packets,
one blue, one white.
Walks between the ramrodded rows
scattering his seed into my neat trenches.
I cover it quickly as the blackbird
watches from the naked plum tree.

One summer's evening after our silent meal
I hold my breath
while father embarks on his nightly inspection.
In the white lobelia row
a flash of blue defiance.
I tell him nature has its aberrations;
try to explain the complicated science of genetics.
'Don't give me that claptrap. Science, my arse.'

The blackbird sings plum-drunk in the twilight.

Cyberspeak

Out there they speak another language
Brutal
No pleasantries or modifiers
The language of imperatives
No conditionals
No ifs and buts
No softeners
Please
and thank-yous.

Deadly reductionism:
Drag
Drop.
The little mouse does their dirty work:
Select
Enter
Execute.

White Dreams

In white dreams
virgins see themselves
visions in satin and lace:
baby's breath breathes
gently upon them.

They float down heavenly aisles
joyful; ethereal:
angel choirs drown out
their fears.

Where are their suitors?
Those callow, spotty youths
loud in flannelette
breathing beery breath
swearing blue curses.

They are closing in on their quarry.

Dali Suite

'…just because I don't know the meaning of my art, does not mean it has no meaning' – Salvador Dali

Salvador has formed me
as a rhombus in this raw
angled room; placed fleshlight
on my left calf muscle; raised
razored.
For the rest
he has smoothed me with the blunt
edge of his knife; coiled my hair
three arabesques
curved me into cerulean space.
Open window.
A ladder of panes.
Rungs   I cannot climb.

*

The room is still raw from last night
but the day is without a wound.
This time of day is best.
It's all about water.
I think of when we went hand-in-hand,
free to walk the jagged mountains
found wild hyacinths,
moist amid the blades.   *Blue*.

*

I ask Salvador to paint me blue;
read to him from lapis lazuli
illuminated manuscripts;
show him jewellery of seastones:
aquamarine, sapphire, turquoise
tumble; take him to a secret meadow:
sunlight violets, dry campanulas
moonsweet.
Salvador spears the watery sky
mixes moist hyacinth
with an argent dawn
soft
like faded doveskin
or the inside of an oyster shell.

Then   he paints me.

Salvador Dali, *Muchacha en la ventana* (1925)

Take off your jacket

'It's the jacket that makes you unapproachable;
keeps customers at a distance. What Management wants,
what will turn this company around, is for you
to take off your jacket.

Get the customer up close and personal,
he has to feel he's your friend.
That way, he'll trust you.
In shirt sleeves, you look as if you can get

your hands dirty.' Your father went to work
in overalls, came home filthy
as his father had before. Grandad
washed off all the coal dust in a hip bath,

Grandma filled from a tap in the yard,
then heated on the wood stove.
The bosses at the coal pit wouldn't pay him
to wash on their time. Their muck

taken off in his time.
When his grandson told him he wore a suit to work,
the old man knew they'd broken through.
So, when the boss orders his grandson to take off his jacket,

what he's saying is 'Take off the respect you have earned.
Take off the years of grind and education.
Put back the grovel. Take off your jacket.
Remember you are one of them.   Not one of us.'

Disapproval

You hate the Soviet Union
scorn painted fingernails
women who smoke.
Loathe cocktails;
deplore frivolous hats.
A burst of jazz could give you a seizure;
I wish it would.

Whistling Shrimps

'The abandonment of Marx, Engels, and Lenin – those who wait for that must wait until a shrimp learns to whistle.' – Nikita Kruschev

I hear a sound on the breeze
I hear a whisper in the trees
Spreading out across the seas

All the shrimps have learned to whistle.

Destruction of the Species

Sleeping wombat, tucked up quietly in your highway bed
your face gentle in repose, no marks visible.
You won't wake soon and shamble off back to your hole.
Sleep soundly little bear.

Vombatus ursinus.
Forty thousand years ago a diprotodon walked this way,
but it's gone too and you are on your way to join him.
One of the fallen. Heavy.
Grave with grief.

Quick, quick brown fox jump over the lazy wombat.
Too late.
Now you too are stopped red in your tracks.
Vulpes Vulpes, some call you a pest.
Not your fault little fox. They brought you here.
The only field you knew was a paddock.
Already Mr Corvus and company caw
over your spoilt body.

The other side too counts its losses.
The highway is an unquiet graveyard for them,
crosses, plastic flowers, ribbons and soft toys
mark those spaces where souls have sped.
No food for crows.

At Darfur

I am a nobody of nothingness.
A woman at the dried-up well waiting
for water; frantic for a grainy hand-out.
Soldiers jab my spine
nerve end of metal.
Children cling to my skirt;
hook me with their eyes,
I pleat them to me
braiding their cries with mine.
Give me a voice.
Say I matter
on the lip of this earth.

At the Liberty Hotel

Take One: On the pavement
'It's cappuccino time.
Catch the mood,' yells Bruno, the director.
Idlers linger.
Someone strikes a match
a jumbo jet
trails the sordid sky.

Take Two: Penthouse Suite
Old cowboy shooting the odds
'Got cable? I want the Rodeo channel…
Now ya hear?'

Take Three: Near the Elevator
Porter unshaven and seedy
battles an overloaded luggage trolley,
spills a small pigskin vanity.

Take Four: Room 1001
'Jeez! Is this your best room?'
Skye's soon gulping coke and snorting.
Her favourite radio station blares out
Country and Western full bore,
Donna Fargo sings 'Daddy'.

Take Five: Hotel Kitchen
A Yugoslav refugee
lights a cigarette.
'My name is Marek
I come from Bosnia
my country
She is finished.'
He flicks the centrefold
Skye is there,
All-American Doll.

Take Six: The Elevator
Seedy porter speeds skywards
his fingers leave sweaty imprints
on the pigskin vanity.

Take Seven: Room Service
Marek prepares a lonely fruit plate.

Take Eight: The Service Elevator
Marek steps into the service lift,
[Hand-held camera follows: nervous jerky movement]
Figs and brie for company.

Take Nine: Outside Room 1001
They arrive together
pigskin vanity and lonely fruit plate.
Marek knocks;
seedy porter coughs discreetly,
vanity at the ready.
The door swings open;
dust motes swirl
at the unlocked window.

Take Ten: Penthouse Suite
Old cowboy loosens his belt
hangs up his holster
empties his barrel
The rodeo has begun.

Food of Love

'I don't give a fig,' says Adam to Eve.
She is silent thinking
of the small orifice on the fruit
a narrow passage for the fig wasp to enter;
set down eggs; pollinate the flowery fig.
Bloom and ripen.
She reveals none of this to Adam
who shields his manhood with a leaf from the fig;
seething at his ejection from the Garden.

Eve isn't sorry that she bit
into the temptation of the fruit;
found its secret self.
She never forgot that first taste
of paradise; brought the knowledge with her
beyond the garden into the world of weeds and thorns.
Of course Adam put it about
it was the snake's clever lies that had beguiled her.
She was deceived (he said). Eve knew better.
She had bloomed. Ripened; tasted truth.

On Figs

'You have become invisible like the fig flower' – Bengali proverb

Fig
greening,
sweetening,
before the knife
unpeels fig wasps
fuming
without a sting
inside its bronze fuzzed
inflorescence.

'Figs are beginning to ripen' – Song of Songs 2:13

In the slow Mediterrane black Tellanian figs
older than grain have quickened again
in the Centurion's walled garden.
Since his last campaign, he has raised
snow white geese with sharp yellow bills;
makes a fine minced dish of fig-fattened
livers. (A skill he learned off an old soldier in Gaul.)
He stains bread hot from the clay oven
with wine blood-red, spreads the duck liver paste;
savours the sweet secrecy of the fig.

Nine sub fossil figs found in the early Neolithic village Gilgal 1 in the Jordan Valley dated to about 9400–9200 BC

Nine thousand years Before Christ; thirteen kilometres from Jericho
Joshua plays his trumpet; the Israelites eat figs until the walls fall down.
2000 Anno Domini on the West Bank, Arab and Jewish settlers fire missiles;
stop their children's songs with old wrongs; lean their rocket carriers
against the trunks of ancient figs; pick up plough shares; bury their innocents.
Peace, like the fig flower, is invisible.

Poussins

Ned brings the Cornish hens to her kitchen door.
He's wrung their necks; they hang like bloody rags
From his fingers – life punched out of them.
The boy's square knuckles scarlet as if he's been
In a fight and come off worse, 'Too 'ot,' he mutters.
She pulls out their lights, tosses them to Tabby
Cat who eats, delicately, a pink worm
Entrail caught in his soft paw. Velvet.

Afterwards, Tabby cleans himself;
Jumps; hunches on the white plaster sill
Beside a blue Wedgwood jug massed
Sunflowers. His eyes mosses
Soaking the afternoon sun.
Tabby hears the gate creak. Footsteps.

Cordon Bleu

Cheese from Iberico; a scent of fresh figs,
And four dead birds. Poussins.
A fancy name for a Cornish hen.
All my recipes are in my head.
I wipe, quarter the figs
with a silver-handled paring knife;
Push the blade
Deep into their purple bulge
Prod, poke, as delicately as Tabby cat
Does with the hens' innards I toss him.
(Once I'd bitten into a fig, found a spit of a wasp
Caught.) I sprinkle five spice powder;
Pour a vintage port wine, I've had Ned fetch from the cellar,
He's wiped free the fuzz of dead flies
Trapped in the glue of a web.
Down on a bed of rock salt I lay the hens,
Not quite touching. My silver knife loosens
Their skins. I stuff the blue-black squelching
Mass of the fig beneath the slip of the Cornish hens' skin.
There: my secret.

Of course it was over

Their last meal together was Poussins
stuffed with Tellanian figs
blue-black aromatic

mess of fecundity.
Their smell and the roast of hens
brought him to her table,

his eyebrow raised enquiring;
his mouth pliant.
Suddenly, she knew she wanted him

out of her kitchen prodded him
with the silver-handled paring knife
Sent him on his way:

with a hunk of Iberico cheese,
and some fig wafers
to begin the long journey back to himself.

Voyages

Go, go, go, said the bird
 T.S Eliot, 'Burnt Norton', from *Four Quartets*

En route to Alaska

The sun wakes me at sea
Vancouver Island to my left;

to my right mocha seals
bask on mottled rocks.

Sitka spruces a dark mystery
– the Rockies a snow of alabaster;

sky and sea are celestine and silver.
Out here in the blind of morning,

I squint through binoculars and see
a bald eagle hook himself to hemlock.

His head looks like a tennis ball thrown
high into the morning air by a careless child.

Riding the cable car

Outside Macey's, a woman wearing spectacles
and a clean hairstyle like a small-town librarian
sits on the sidewalk – holds a cardboard sign
handwritten: 'I have breast cancer.
Health cover running low.'

On Union, I gape at slender houses
zigzagged fire escapes, art deco frescoed
– they look like houses I want to live in.

Down at the Wharf, a joyful beggar shakes
the noise of dimes and quarters.
Crabs seethe pink in vats of boiling water.
You say, 'Death is something we're always dealing with.'

Fog moves in like a hustler, his clutch
icy around my neck
I wince; wind my scarf,
green and watery as a mermaid's tail.

At the King Memorial, a veil of water falls
Martin Luther's voice rails
Pure glass his words wash me clean.
'Justice rolls down like water.
Righteousness like a mighty stream.'

Our driver booms, 'Don't lean out.'

Tug of War Waikiki

In Queen Kapi'olani Park last Saturday
I watched a tug of war
between a giant of a boy at one end of a twisted rope
and half a dozen boys at the other.
The giant was good-natured,
wrapped the rope around his girth,
laughing; he expected to win.
He did.
Easily.
With one swift tug.
Then something wonderful happened.
The losers were joined by a young woman
wearing a white dress with red hibiscus flowers:
three boys in white shorts;
mothers and fathers,
laughing, holding small babies
took hold of the rope.
The losers numbers doubled
then more.
The giant beamed,
fastened the rope again
around his wide girth;
still smiling was brought to his knees.
With one swift tug.

Victoria Falls

There are always men who want to race lions.
Even here, where white water falls

long and deep into the Zambezi.
They risk everything for the glory of their race;

sacrifice themselves for Queen and Country.
They do this to feel the weight of brass, pinned

heavy on their breasts. Each wants to be fêted
at banquets; to rise above the noise

of cheers; stand tall among them all.
Tell how they set about racing lions.

I think of what you said to me by the baobab tree
'This country belongs to the lion.

One began to follow your footprints half an hour
after you passed here, yesterday.'

I wonder, will I make it back to where the Falls
steam and hiss at the top or will mine and the lion's

path cross somewhere further up the track?
Will he wait to make my acquaintance?

Anzac Day at Moruya

'Childhood is the kingdom where nobody dies' – Edna St Vincent Millais

The Light Horse Re-enactment: gun carriage,
four chestnut horses, riders dressed as Anzacs,
khaki, slouch hats with feathers sweeps into Page Street.
A brass band blows 'Lead Kindly Light' over the dusty town.

Vintage cars roll up, old soldiers stagger; steady;
fall in. Returned service men and women grip flags.
Boy scouts, sea scouts, track-suited walkers
clutch medals. Children clasp their parents' hands.
Teenagers uniformed, ear-ringed are at ease.

Major General (Retired), scornful of the microphone,
squares his shoulders remembers,
Our generation did a good job.
Jack dances a jig. *I'm busting.*

The bugle plays 'The Last Post' then 'Reveille'.
A marcher topples to the ground. The band strikes up
'Abide with Me'. An ambulance, lights blazing,
siren muted, scatters the crowd.
When other helpers fail and comforts flee.

Going home, Kate asks, *What does fail mean?*

Goosegreen

Tommy Lennon was a merchant seaman and an amateur boxer who was killed in the Falklands War (1982). His ship was hit by an Exocet missile.

Tommy Lennon fought off all comers;
won that night at the Nottingham Goose Fair.
No room in this ring for hand-to-hand combat
He will never smell the sawdust;
feel the heat of stinking bodies and market lights.
Only smells the cordite now.
Blinded by the flashes of hurtling missiles
Never feels the blow aimed below the belt
Notes with some part of his being that
        His lights went out.

In the High Country

On the snowline a scramble of gums
Trunks rinsed with the memory of blood,
Prepares for another bout with the tyranny of weather.
Today's a truce. Quiet as the poison farmers
Pushed deep into the earth.
Quiet as a billy-button's yellow fist,
A pugilist's whispered threat or the hush of snow.
Quiet as a pygmy possum in the whorled palm of my hand.

I think of explorations: men with maps wrapped in pigskin;
Din of shovel; thud of pick – the rush of miners to claim
Colour under a lunatic sky. A crow calls below.
Thredbo looks like a toy town guarded by an anxious
Child waiting for the school bully to pounce,
Knock him down and jump on it.

Detainees

(Queens Park, Invercargill, South Island, NZ)

The prisoner in solitary
sulphur crest secured
hides sunlight beneath his wings.

Pure as an archangel
feigning feathered sleep
eyes shuttered down blind.

Through the wire, I whisper warm
scent of gum days; leaves that stink,
oily heat.   He lifts

the white blind of sleep
opens an eye dark, deep as an inky fjord
where water falls as white smoke

memory of that other place wheeling wide
iron sky. The noise of birds at dawn and dusk
screaming murder.

The dumbness of blunt rock;
the bigness of that other land
the way it all can't be known unlike

this prison park lovingly assembled
a map of winding paths – where he is a caged exhibit.
The sign reads, *Cacatua galerita. Careful, he bites.*

At the edge of the world
sunlight glares;
air knocks like a fist.

He and I locked down together
in the arctic, white cold bite of summer.

Kaka

(Queens Park, Invercargill, South Island, NZ)

Mocking sunlight casts
upon the ceiling of his cage
a mirror of himself.
An age he's been locked up
Freedom, a lonely memory.
Mountain air, wheeling flight
Lost birthright.
He hops now side to side
Dull-eyed.
Shadows fall.
His other self lengthens
Slides slowly down the wall.

Kea

(Queens Park, Invercargill, South Island, NZ)

Warning: Do not feed the kea

They've put the big boys in solitary.
This one's heavy of feather, bronze chain mail
Disdainful of his cage – a man-made jail,
Imprisoned for delinquency.

Fierce of beak; consumed by villainy
His exploits leave a trail
Of destruction on a monumental scale.
Lock him up and throw away the key.

He refuses rehabilitation. Won't be tamed.
Will not mend his ways – remains defiant:
Militant, obdurate, miscreant.
Brags his innocence unashamed,

He lifts the iron curtain of his wing
Blazes sunset fire on everything.

The Weight of Trees

(for June Foster)

Two fires burn fierce
in a room full of party,
June and her professor

are leaving for the suburbs.
Ladies sip sweet sherry
men down beers and peddle

stories. June speaks of trees
Charles Weston's exotics.
'Today I saw two lindens

at University House.
Linden tree of legend:
lovers' leaves, yielding hearts,

honeyed, bowered blossom.
Icons are painted on
its supple yellow wood.

Lindens live a thousand years.'
June and her professor
hold hands; tell of a bed.

Double. 'We went to Goulburn,
'to buy it,' they said and
can't wait for its delivery.

Ned's born nine months later.
Five others follow all
planted in the suburbs

with a chinese elm.
June and her professor
light bonfires with its leaves.

(The Fireside Room, Gorman House, Government Hostel Canberra, c. 1951)

A Tolstoy Reader in Melbourne

A girl with wide-apart eyes
skin like sieved sand reads
Tolstoy on the Skybus.
What does she make of it all
the train and the troika;
the mess of their lives?

Has Vronsky's horse Frou Frou
thrown them into a frenzy yet?
Has she got to the part where Anna leaves
her worthy husband, Karenin whose
name in Russian means head?

Anna wants fire not cold reason.
She will not compromise
or divide herself.
Anna is all for Vronsky
that dashing rat!

And what does the girl with wide-apart eyes
think about Lenin and his logic?
He won't let Kitty say, 'I do'
until she's read his journals.
What a man he is in his peasant
smock; smiting the air with his principles

What of Kitty's sister, Dolly
and that husband of hers
and all his affairs?
It's all too much.
Anna's head is turned so far
she cannot turn it back.
She places it on the track.

The girl with wide-apart eyes
reads on and on we move.
The train and the troika;
the mess of our lives.

Trespassers

(for Brian)

The best of both worlds you say: a long walk
over the moor with a beer at the end of it.
We cross over a wooden footbridge into a field.
At home we'd call it a paddock.

The weather is giving us the benefit
of the doubt, but rain soon falls.
At first, no more than a nuisance,
until the sky lowers as if it would press us

between ploughed earth and iron sky.
We climb over the first stile into another field
full of white sheep; the rain comes at us sideways
– it's rain designed to get rid of trespassers.

At home, this much wet would be a blessing
drought breaking rain. We'd give thanks
as galahs performed grateful aerobatics,
perched on wires above our parched gardens.

Here no birds play.
Behind a crooked stone wall, ancient;
crudely put together, we huddle.
Sheep shelter with us looking intelligent.

If they could speak, I think they'd say,
Why aren't you in your dry house
keeping warm? We push on to the pub
two humans in a sodden world

swimming in a flooded field.
When we clamber over the second stile,
a church spire points the way we have to go.
At The Rising Sun, a large sign is pinned

to the pub's oak door. The ink is blurred;
there is no mistaking the purpose
and intent of black ink strokes,
'Walkers not welcome here'.

Evening Boat Ride on the Moruya River

Light slow marches
across the river bank,
a column of ghost soldiers
surrendering to the night.

Light liquefies on water.
Sparking energy
bursting before the dark.

As we plane light and water,
three black swans,
necks outstretched
push home.

Mysteries

'Quick said the bird, find them, find them.'
T.S. Eliot, 'Burnt Norton', from *Four Quartets*

A History of Birds

(for Jonathan)

Last night, we brought the dead back to life.
Words sly with red wine slipped into the friendly
dark and smoothed out our untidy pasts.

In the old photograph, Peggy
in her wedding dress; her groom
the roughness of his khaki.

We read her careful copperplate –
'Wedding Day May 1942.'

This morning, a wattle bird takes flight
framed by the breakfast light
of the sycamore tree.

The language of the bird is the curve
& dance of my pen. My hand is a bird
moving, turning,
                              joining, marking.

Birds write nothing of themselves.

trust

for VE

1.

The pardalote is very still
cold on the footpath. The man
buries it in the breast pocket

of his old tweed coat, carries home
his weekly shopping: two green bags
filled with today's specials.

He feels a throb of tweed – the bird
feathers its small nest. At home,
he stands devout as a cathedral

beneath the apricot tree –
pardalote held on
his outstretched palm.

2.

Unblinking. The hare is safe
in the sanctuary of man's shadow.

Unseen. Man's eyes seek
mysteries beyond the fundamentals

of earth and mountain; beyond
the menace of two eagles hunting

yellow bellies exposed;
trailing the noose of legs and feet.

The hare turns its face to man,
feels the wheel of eagles' wings.

Vault of sky; spire of man;
tremble of the hare.

3.

Amidst a snare of starlings, a swift
gobble-mouthed as a gargoyle

fights for life. The man steps forward,
picks it up; settles the bird

on his shoulder. The entire
journey home it gives curious

commuters its steady swift stare;
stays put on the sanctuary

of shoulder. Up a flight of stairs
a room beneath the eaves – the man's

infant rests in a nest of sleep.
At the open window, the swift scents

release of air   up,   up   swings;
soars above the shingle of red roofs.

The man locks the window,
draws the blind closed,
bends to the sleeping child.

Mothers Day

While they talk on
of stock markets & retirement strategies,
I examine a gelato cloud above me.

Colours sift through peppermint,
watermelon, blueberry blue.
You sent it instead of a bouquet

to remind me of ice cream days
of motherhood.
They talk on as the cloud drifts by,

I want to tell them, 'Look, look.'
But now it's talk of gold shares.
There's gold all around.

It's a golden day.
I saw a flame robin this morning
burning against the blue.

I want to say to you
boy turned man
don't expect so much.

Unclench your fingers, take
stock: this day will end soon;
night comes swiftly.

It may be a cruel one.

Singing Girl

Childhood trains you into the tunnel
choo-chooing cradle songs.
Points change. You switch track. Whiz!
You're grown smart as sunshine.

On a railway platform you wait
for your favourite lover to arrive.
Your lemon cardigan stretched
tight across your breasts. His train's late,

(in fact, it never arrives.)

Leaving behind a trail of mother-
of-pearl buttons, you board the next
Express. It roars you into the tunnel.
You jazz the light soft

like a new century's sunrise.
Harmonising.
The tunnel ends; you are out the other side.
Razzamatazzing the dark.

76 Birkhall Road

You can't see me sitting here on this boulder.
A marker from a major extinction event
smeared with lichen; tarnished with dead moss.
Behind me is a thorn tree stripped bare
it looks like someone has wrapped
barbed wire around its trunk.
You were my marker along with the brick-red door,
a number 'seventy-six,' and a small crack
in the bubbled glass of a door frame.
Look. There's the rose Dad planted for you.
When it blooms, it's the colour of old blood.

When I hear the magpie carol,
I am a child again, at home
in the light; looking out
on to that dark Yorkshire field.
Dad's in the kitchen: turning on taps,
knocking crockery, banging pans,
clicking cupboard doors shut.
Chris is in the cherry-red rocking chair
watching an episode of *The Fugitive*.
John and Judy play a dumb show,
stifle giggles because baby is asleep
his bottle fallen from his hand.
Milk pools in the cracks of the leather sofa
drips on to the scuffed green carpet.

The coal fire settles to a garnet of heat.
I am eleven years old and you are not here.
Outside the road is a shadow of sodium light.
Snow lays fast.
Tomorrow, we'll make long slides
annoy the neighbours.
Tonight, there is the shivery bark of a neighbour's dog
needing to be let in.

Our Family Tree

And another thing, my mother said
and threw her stick. It landed dead
in the middle of the front room,
just missing the old brown sofa
and sprouted a tree with no name
botanical or otherwise.

It flourished fruit at Christmastime.
Sweet. We gorged until we were sick.
Green leaves shaded us from summer's heat;
we rested from cannon-ball and cricket:
nursed grazed knees, twisted ankles; and worse
once a broken elbow.

Autumn, it dropped leaves – slippery,
An accident waiting to happen, my mother said.
It nearly died that first winter when we left.
Only fit for firewood.
But, last time I was home, my mother said,
A blackbird flew in this morning
I can't get it out.
I looked and saw its black flutter
in our family tree.
'It's nesting,' I said,
Then, late one afternoon mid-August,
the blackbird took my mother's hand,
Time to go, it said.

Wintergrief

The years I spent away
I wintered,
burying passion bulb-deep
letting it lie.
I withered
withdrew to
winterspace
where knifed by dry-eyed wind
I withstood
winterhood.

It seems he was loved until that moment

'Often there is an act of love behind abandonment' – Dr Piermichele Paolillo*

She finger presses his flannel nightgown soft,
fastens a cloth napkin fresh around his powdered cheeks,
smiles a last time at his small clawings;

inhales the nape of his neck feathered
like a nest and tastes the fold behind his ear.
There hasn't been time for it to be smoothed

or straightened – she shawls him neatly like a bird;
covers his mouth with hers one last time
and would take him back inside herself

if only she could.
Her mouth is bruised with the mystery of all this.
He feels the brevity of maternity

his fingers reach for her breast for one final suckling.
He does not want to be let go; seems to know
the enormity of her action and that in some future time

he will strive to recapture her.
The liquid that was his mother.

* *New York Times*, 28 February 2007

Soft Day

Soft day sensual
like silk wound fondly
around lissom limbs.
Sunlight soaking
violets.
Everywhere sounds
silence.
Bees hugger-mugger
wet roses.
Blue wrens flit space
twitting; worrying
wild wisteria
framing sky.
Soft day.

Prayer Bird

The king parrot eats from my open palm.
Eyes circled – two golden rings
worn thin after a long marriage.

He peals a bell; brings a call to prayer.
The Angelus bell brought my father
to his knees. Each day, he fingered

beads; dropped an Ave from his lips.
My father's prayer lifted, drifted
through the open casement window,

hovered above the field, where I played
summer games. My father's prayer
rose above our town and the filth of industry

that settled black on his lungs.
My father's prayer white as a seraphim's
wing feather soared,

above the purple, heathered moor;
circled the grey metal of the North Sea.
        Leavening.

www.ingramcontent.com/pod-product-compliance
Lightning Source LLC
Chambersburg PA
CBHW062145100526
44589CB00014B/1693